Things to Know
about Paintings

Happy House

About Wise & Wide

- A systematic 6-level English reading program based on Lexile® measures
- Diverse and interesting topics chosen from the elementary curriculums of Korea and English speaking western countries
- Well-written books in various forms including fiction stories, descriptive texts, and classics retold
- The informative but original fiction stories grab your interest, leading to the easy and clear understanding of the educational content.
- Improve thinking skills with solid after-reading activities at all levels of the series.

Wise & Wide is a 6-level English reading program that consists of 60 books and each level is systematically divided by Lexile® measures. The Lexile® Framework for Reading is the most popular reading measuring system in American formal education curriculums and many English programs. Over 20 out of 50 states in the U.S. mark Lexile® measures directly on students' final report cards and over 300 well-known publishers adopt and use Lexile® measures.

Experience many kinds of readings written by professional writers from the U.S. and England. They used interesting topics that were carefully chosen after analyzing elementary curriculums from around the world including Korea, the U.S., England, and Australia among many others. Comprehensive after-reading activities including graphic organizers, speaking tasks, and After-reading Tests are ready for you.

Levels in the series and their corresponding Lexile® measures

Level	Lexile® measures	U.S. Grade
Level 1	Below 200L	Pre K - K
Level 2	190L - 400L	Lower Grade 1
Level 3	350L - 530L	Upper Grade 1
Level 4	420L - 650L	Grade 2
Level 5	520L - 940L	Grade 3 - 4
Level 6	830L - 1070L	Grade 5 - 6

* Smart Readers: Wise & Wide level 1 is applicable to the preschool level in the U.S.
* The source of the relationship between Lexile® measures and U.S. school grades: CCSS(Common Core State Standards) FOR ENGLISH LANGUAGE ARTS, APPENDIX A (2012, which is used by 45 states in the U.S.)

Topic List

	Level 1	Level 2	Level 3	Level 4	Level 5	Level 6
Book 1	Science>Biology: The hibernation of animals Story	Science>Biology: Living and nonliving things Story	Science>Biology> Animals & the Environment: Sea otters Story	Environment> Living with nature: The diver & the persimmon tree Story	Science>Biology> Animal: Amazing animals of the Amazon Story	Science>Biology: Germs, transmitted diseases Story
Book 2	Literature> World classics: Aesop's fables Story	Literature> Traditional fairy tale: Old tales about stones Story	Social Studies> Economy: To run a business to make and save money Story	Science>Biology> Plants: Photosynthesis Story	Science>Earth science: Earth's layers, earthquakes, volcanoes, and earth's atmosphere Report	Mathematics> Sequence: The golden ratio & the Fibonacci sequence Story
Book 3	Science>Physics: How shadows are formed Story	Literature> World classics: Peter Pan Story	Science>Scientific technology: Nanobots Story	Literature>Myths: World's creation stories Story	Literature> Legend: The story of King Arthur Story	Literature>Myths: Constellation myths Story
Book 4	Literature> Traditional literature: The Talmud Story	Science>Biology> Animal: Polar bears Story	Science>Biology> Animal: Mountain gorillas Story	Social Studies> Cultural anthropology: Amazing ancient cultures of the world Story	Science> Earth science: Clouds and weather Story	Literature> Human & animals: The friendship between a girl and a horse Story
Book 5	Social Studies> Ethics: Rules in daily life Story	Science>Biology: The five senses Report	Social Studies> Cultural anthropology: Astonishing festivals Report	Art>Music: Stories from two operas Story	Social Studies> World culture & history: The Renaissance Story	Sports> Board sports: Surfing & snowboarding Story
Book 6	Social Studies> World geography & travel: Tourist attractions around the world Story	Science>Biology> Animal: Dinosaurs Story	Science> Astronomy: The solar system Story	Social Studies> People: Three great people who overcame hardships Story	Science>Scientific technology: The wonderful world of robots Report	Art>Music: Composers of the Romantic Era Report
Book 7	Science> Space science: The life of astronauts Report	Social Studies> Cultural anthropology: Mythological monsters from around the world Report	Mathematics> Elementary mathematics: Numbers, measurement, shapes and data Report	Science & Social Studies> Technology & culture: Inventions from around the world Report	Art>Works of art: Famous paintings Report	Social Studies> Human & animals: Animals in action for human Report
Book 8	Social Studies> Cultural anthropology: Various living cultures of the world Story	Art>Music: Instruments in the orchestra Story	Social Studies> Life safety: Learning and using outdoor survival skills Story	Social Studies> History: The California Gold Rush Report	Social Studies & Science> Psychology: Psychology in everyday life Story	Literature> World classics: The Merchant of Venice Story
Book 9	Social Studies> Jobs: Interviews about jobs Report	Science>Scientific technology: Developments in technology in different times Story	Social Studies> Politics>Election: Running for 3rd grade class president Story	Literature> World classics: Stories of Sherlock Holmes Story	Literature> World classics: Adrift in the Pacific Story	Social Studies> History & People: Great world leaders in history Report
Book 10	Literature>Traditional fairy tale: Eastern and Western folk tales on the same theme Story	Sports>Winter sports: Various aspects of some Winter Olympic sports Report	Literature> World classics: Short stories by O. Henry Story	Sports> Ball games: Various aspects of popular ball games Report	Social Studies> History: Famous events that changed world history Report	Art & Social Studies> Art: Stories about the creation, distribution, and preservation of paintings Report

10 books in each level will be published.

How to Use This Book

•Before Reading

You can easily find the topic and what kind of story you are about to read.

•The text

All the stories were written by professional writers from the U.S. and England, so you will read authentic and appropriate English sentences and expressions in every book in the series.

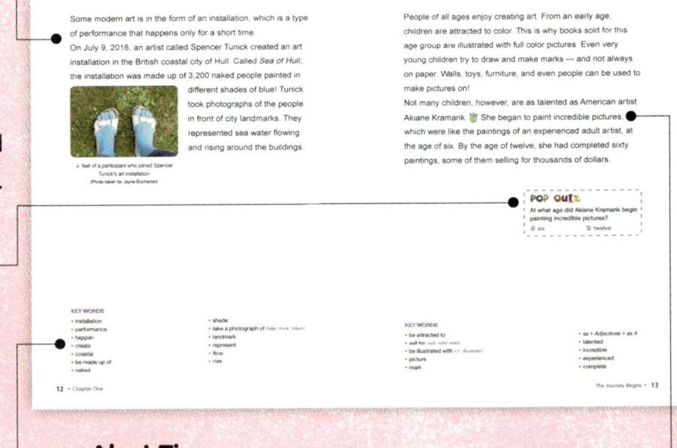

•Pop Quiz

Check out right away if you understand what you have just read by solving a pop quiz that checks your comprehension.

•Key Words

The key words and expressions on each page are listed for you to easily study them.

•Aha! Tips

Download free Korean explanations at *www.ihappyhouse.co.kr* for all of the sentences marked with "Aha!". These explain cultural, scientific, and economic knowledge or they deal with aspects of English such as grammatical structures or idiomatic expressions. There are lots of "Aha! Tips" to help you understand the text.

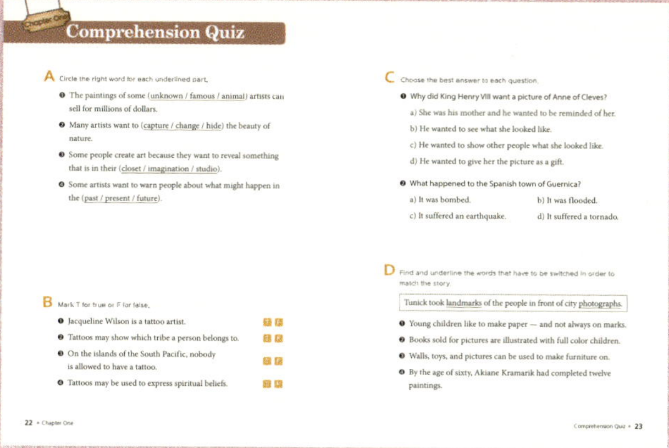

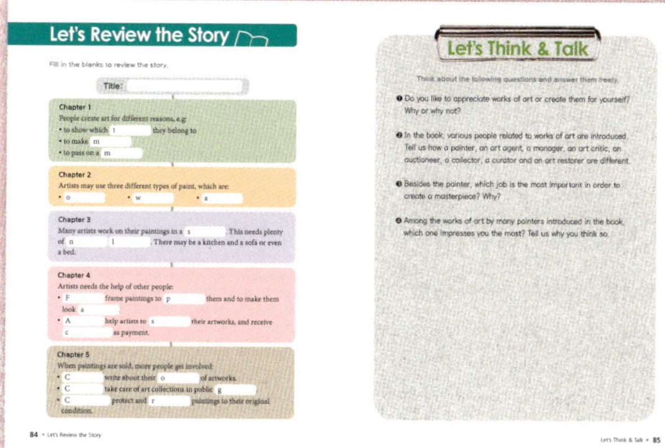

Appendix

Audio CD

In the CD audio book form, the texts are read vividly by American professional voice actors. (MP3 files downloaded for free)

After-reading Test

Solve an additionally provided After-reading Test for each book.

The Korean translation, Answer Keys, a Word Quiz, a Word List, and Aha! Tips for each book

You can download them for free at *www.ihappyhouse.co.kr* or *www.darakwon.co.kr*

Before Reading

Things to Know about Paintings

Level 6–10, Lexile® 950L

- Art & Social Studies〉Art
- Report

Paintings and humans

The Altamira cave paintings in Spain are well-known as the earliest human paintings. A girl entered a cave to find her lost dog and found animal paintings which had been drawn on the wall tens of thousands years ago. Then the public saw them. These cave paintings are famous because they are more detailed and artistic than other prehistoric cave paintings. They show that men have created paintings for a very long time and they have tried to improve their paintings, making them more beautiful and realistic. As time went by and technology developed, people started to create paintings using more varied materials, more advanced drawing techniques and better drawing materials. Through paintings, people can exchange messages even though they use different languages or don't know how to read. They can even read the mind of the painter who lived hundreds of years ago. They can be impressed by outstanding paintings and entertained by interesting paintings as well. Like this, paintings are a big part of human history.

Summary

What are needed for us to appreciate a work of art? First of all, we need a painter to create a work of art. From a prehistoric man a very long time ago to a painting prodigy in the present, we will learn many people create works of art for different reasons. It is not easy for a painter to create a painting. First, the painter has to decide what to draw and what drawing materials to use before creating a painting. Especially, the main painting materials, the paints, have to be chosen carefully as they have different characteristics depending on their type, so the results can be very different depending on which paints are chosen. If the subject and drawing materials are decided, the work can start. Now, the painter needs a suitable studio to create the painting in. We will peek into various painters' studios and check out their working styles. If a work of art is completed, is it over? Amazingly, even after the painter has finished his work, the public needs many people's help in various fields in order to appreciate a work of art. Then, from the painter and his or her work to the related people after the completion of the work, let's find out everything about the journey of a painting.

Contents

Things to Know about Paintings

Things to Know about Paintings

The Journey Begins

What exactly is art? Is it any drawing or painting? Of course not — there are many other forms of art, including sculpture, photography, textiles, and ceramics.

Modern art is displayed at the Tate Modern Gallery in London. Over the years, it has included piles of bricks, giant slides and a hall filled with millions of ceramic sunflower seeds!

▲ a gallery in the Tate Modern Gallery

In an episode of the TV series *The Simpsons*, Homer tries — and fails — to make a barbecue out of scrap metal. 🌐 But it is mistaken for a piece of modern art and displayed for the public to view.

KEY WORDS

- journey
- exactly
- art
- drawing
- form
- including (*cf.* include)
- sculpture
- textile
- ceramic
- modern
- display

- over the years
- pile
- slide
- filled with
- seed
- episode
- barbecue
- scrap metal (*cf.* scrap)
- mistake for (mistake-mistook-mistaken)
- the public
- view

Some modern art is in the form of an installation, which is a type of performance that happens only for a short time.

On July 9, 2016, an artist called Spencer Tunick created an art installation in the British coastal city of Hull. Called *Sea of Hull*, the installation was made up of 3,200 naked people painted in different shades of blue! Tunick took photographs of the people in front of city landmarks. They represented sea water flowing and rising around the buildings.

▲ feet of a participant who joined Spencer Tunick's art installation

(Photo taken by Jayne Buchanan)

KEY WORDS

- installation
- performance
- happen
- create
- coastal
- be made up of
- naked

- shade
- take a photograph of (take-took-taken)
- landmark
- represent
- flow
- rise

People of all ages enjoy creating art. From an early age, children are attracted to color. This is why books sold for this age group are illustrated with full color pictures. Even very young children try to draw and make marks — and not always on paper. Walls, toys, furniture, and even people can be used to make pictures on!

Not many children, however, are as talented as American artist Akiane Kramarik. She began to paint incredible pictures, which were like the paintings of an experienced adult artist, at the age of six. By the age of twelve, she had completed sixty paintings, some of them selling for thousands of dollars.

KEY WORDS

- be attracted to
- sell for (sell-sold-sold)
- be illustrated with (cf. illustrate)
- picture
- mark

- as + *Adjectives* + as A
- talented
- incredible
- experienced
- complete

▲ a satin bowerbird

▲ blue things that a satin bowerbird
gathered in its nest

Some people believe that even animals create works of art. In Australia, male satin bowerbirds collect blue items and arrange them in structures called "bowers" to attract females. Flowers, pieces of glass, drinking straws, and clothespins have all been found in their carefully built bowers.

The keepers at the St. Louis Zoo in the U.S.A. allow some of their animals to experiment with paints. Snakes, apes, penguins and even insects can make paint marks on canvases. Their artworks are sold to raise money for zoo projects.

KEY WORDS

- satin bowerbird
- item
- arrange
- structure
- bower

- clothespin
- keeper
- allow
- experiment with
- ape

- insect
- artwork
- raise money
- project

People of all cultures create art, and it is an important way to learn about history. Cave paintings date from prehistoric times, up to 40,000 years ago.

▲ a cave painting from prehistoric times

They can be found on most continents. They were painted on cave walls using fingers or simple tools. Colors — or pigments — were made using earth and rocks. This is why most cave paintings are red, black, brown, or yellowish colors. **Aha!**

In the 2013 movie, *The Croods*, a caveman makes pictures on the wall of a cave to tell the story of his family. They were probably also a way of passing on information about which animals lived nearby and how to catch them.

KEY WORDS

- date from
- prehistoric times
- up to
- continent
- tool
- pigment
- earth
- yellowish
- probably (= perhaps)
- pass on (*cf*. pass)
- nearby

In some cultures, people create art on their own bodies in the form of tattoos. You can read about a woman who did this in Jacqueline Wilson's novel for children, *The Illustrated Mum*.

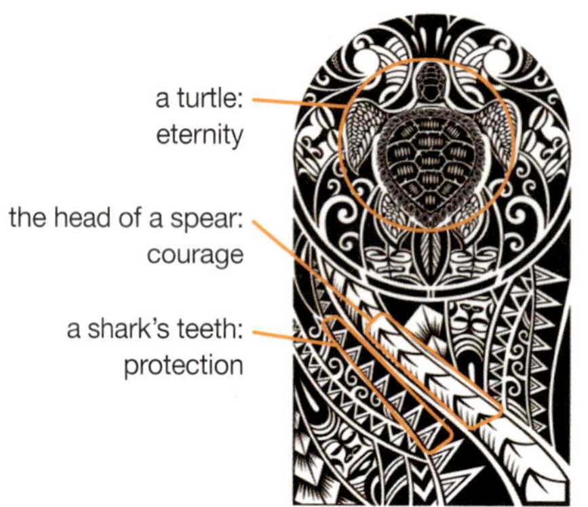

▲ various symbols in tattoos and their meanings

Often, people do it because they like the way it looks. But in some cultures, such as those of the island nations in the South Pacific, these tattooed symbols have important meanings. They may show which family or tribe a person belongs to. They may be used to express religious or spiritual beliefs.

Why else do people create art? Some people do it to make money, like any other job. Before photographs existed, artists painted portraits of people to show what they looked like.

When King Henry VIII was on the throne of England in 1539, he sent the painter Hans Holbein to Germany. Holbein's task was to paint a picture of a young woman called Anne of Cleves. Henry was thinking of marrying her, and he wanted to see what she looked like. This was the only way of showing Henry what she looked like.

▲ a portrait of Henry VIII by Hans Holbein

POP QUIZ

Who painted a portrait of Anne of Cleves?

ⓐ Anne of Cleves
ⓑ Hans Holbein

KEY WORDS

- else
- make money
- exist
- portrait
- look like
- be on the throne of
- task
- Cleves
- marry

▲ a portrait of Anne of Cleves
by Hans Holbein

Holbein produced a pleasant portrait, so Henry agreed to marry her. But when he saw Anne in real life, he said that she looked like a fat horse! Not surprisingly, Holbein was never again asked to produce paintings for the king.

In modern times, photographers take pictures of people, families, and even pets to make money.

The paintings of some famous artists can sell for millions of dollars, although sadly many artists do not become famous until after they are dead.

KEY WORDS

- produce
- pleasant
- in real life
- not surprisingly
- although
- sadly

Many people create art simply because they enjoy it, or because they want to learn something new. They can develop skills and understanding. Perhaps they want to capture the beauty of nature or to try and reveal something that is in their imagination. Perhaps they want to express an emotion such as joy, anger, or sadness.

KEY WORDS

- simply
- develop
- skill
- understanding
- capture
- try and + *Verb* (= try to + *Verb*)
- reveal
- imagination
- emotion

Other people create art because they want to pass on a message. They want to tell a story of something that has happened, or they want to warn people about something that might happen in the future.

For example, Pablo Picasso's famous painting, *Guernica*, was painted after a Spanish town called Guernica was bombed. It records the suffering of the people in that village. It also gives a message to everyone that war is a bad thing.

▲ the town of Guernica after several bombing attacks during the Spanish Civil War

KEY WORDS

- warn
- bomb

- record
- suffering

Art is a way of sharing deep thoughts and emotions in such a way that people who view the art can also experience them. It is a way of bringing people together and making them realize that they are not alone.

So art is basically about communication from one person to another. Let us imagine an artist who has an emotion or a message that he or she wants to share. Let us also picture a viewer who sees the artwork and receives the message. How does the message get passed from one to the other? What other people are involved in passing it on? Let us investigate the journey that paintings take, from beginning to end.

KEY WORDS

- share
- in such a way that
- bring together (bring-brought-brought)
- realize
- basically

- communication
- receive
- be involved in
- investigate

Comprehension Quiz

A Circle the right word for each underlined part.

1. The paintings of some (<u>unknown / famous / animal</u>) artists can sell for millions of dollars.

2. Many artists want to (<u>capture / change / hide</u>) the beauty of nature.

3. Some people create art because they want to reveal something that is in their (<u>closet / imagination / studio</u>).

4. Some artists want to warn people about what might happen in the (<u>past / present / future</u>).

B Mark T for true or F for false.

1. Jacqueline Wilson is a tattoo artist.　　T　F

2. Tattoos may show which tribe a person belongs to.　　T　F

3. On the islands of the South Pacific, nobody is allowed to have a tattoo.　　T　F

4. Tattoos may be used to express spiritual beliefs.　　T　F

 Choose the best answer to each question.

❶ Why did King Henry VIII want a picture of Anne of Cleves?

   a) She was his mother and he wanted to be reminded of her.

   b) He wanted to see what she looked like.

   c) He wanted to show other people what she looked like.

   d) He wanted to give her the picture as a gift.

❷ What happened to the Spanish town of Guernica?

   a) It was bombed.   b) It was flooded.

   c) It suffered an earthquake.   d) It suffered a tornado.

D Find and underline the words that have to be switched in order to match the story.

Tunick took <u>landmarks</u> of the people in front of city <u>photographs</u>.

❶ Young children like to make paper — and not always on marks.

❷ Books sold for pictures are illustrated with full color children.

❸ Walls, toys, and pictures can be used to make furniture on.

❹ By the age of sixty, Akiane Kramarik had completed twelve paintings.

Getting Ready to Paint

How does an artist decide what to paint? Artists get their inspiration from all kinds of different places. Most would agree that ideas can come from anywhere, and when they are least expected!

▲ still life painting

Some artists paint real objects, which may be natural or made by humans. This is called a "still life" painting. The artist seeks to capture a realistic image of something that will not last.

KEY WORDS

- **get ready** (get-got-gotten)
- **decide**
- **inspiration**
- **come from** (*cf.* come)
- **least**
- **expect**

- **object**
- **natural**
- **still life**
- **seek to + *Verb*** (seek-sought-sought)
- **realistic**
- **last**

This is why flowers and fruit were popular choices for still life paintings in the past, before photography was popular, and are still popular choices today. Other artists choose more unusual subjects, such as this painting called *Mound of Butter*. It was painted by French artist Antoine Vallon in the 19th century. Many artists are inspired by nature, whether they choose to paint individual animals or plants or whether they choose to paint landscapes.

Botanical artist Martin J. Allen paints highly detailed paintings of plants. He is inspired by the moment when a flower bud begins to open. This idea of capturing the moment of change inspired a whole collection of paintings exhibited in 1987.

▲ *Mound of Butter* by Antoine Vallon

▲ a work done in the 1880s by a
botanical artist, Charles Antoine

▲ *Guardian Spirit of the Waters*
by Odilon Redon

Some artists are inspired by their dreams. A French artist called Odilon Redon painted what he called "black" pictures, which were made up of images which were in his dreams and nightmares. In 1878, he painted *Guardian Spirit of the Waters*, which contains a face hovering over the sea.

▲ Odilon Redon(1840~1916)

KEY WORDS

- choice
- past
- subject
- mound
- be inspired by (*cf.* inspire)
- whether
- individual
- landscape
- botanical
- highly
- detailed
- bud
- whole
- collection
- exhibit
- nightmare
- guardian spirit
- contain
- face
- hover

▲ an abstract painting by Vasily Kandinsky

Other artists, especially those who paint abstract art (patterns, shapes, and lines with no obvious picture), claim that they get their ideas as they go along. They begin with a feeling, a desire to use a particular color, and then they see how it develops. There is really no limit to where ideas may come from. But once the artist has a strong desire to create, the journey may begin. Aha!

KEY WORDS

- especially
- abstract
- obvious
- claim
- go along (go-went-gone)
- desire
- particular
- limit

Once an artist has decided what image he or she wants to create, the next decisions are the choices of media. An artist must choose what to draw or paint on and what to draw or paint with.

An artist can paint on almost anything. Stone, bark, wood, ceramics, glass, concrete, leather or even the human body are some alternative choices of media. Each of these materials has different properties that may affect how easy or difficult it is to apply paint. They also affect how long the paint will keep its color and appearance.

The artist chooses the medium depending on how the finished piece will look, or what message will be given. For example, an artist may choose to paint on a stone  so that people can pick it up and hold it. The way the rock *feels* may be as important as the way it *looks*.

KEY WORDS

- medium
- bark
- leather
- alternative
- material

- property
- affect
- apply
- **keep** (keep-kept-kept)
- appearance

- depending on
  (*cf.* depend on)
- pick up
- **hold** (hold-held-held)

PASEO DE
LA VIDA

A mural is a picture that is painted directly onto the wall of a building, either inside or outside. Murals can be used to brighten up inner city areas or bare walls. Some street artists paint directly onto sidewalks so that the public can view their work as soon as it is created. There is a particular type of mural or street art called a "trompe l'oeil."  This is French for "mistake of the eye." This is an artwork that forms an illusion or trick. There appears to be a hole in the wall or sidewalk and the viewer sees something completely different beyond.

Graffiti can be a form of art, especially when it is created by world-famous graffiti artist Banksy, who is from England but works all over the world. Nobody knows Banksy's identity, but his works are well known.

▲ graffiti by Banksy

There are many Banksy artworks on walls and buildings in London. Many of them are covered in a transparent plastic called Perspex to protect them. But after a while, some of them are painted over, or the wall on which they are painted is removed. Graffiti art rarely lasts a long time, but you can buy photographs or copies of the paintings to keep.

Many artists choose to paint on a flat surface, which can later be hung on a wall for viewing. In the past, artists mainly used wood for this. Leonardo da Vinci's famous *Mona Lisa*, painted in 1503, was painted on poplar wood. Modern artists usually choose either paper or canvas. The choice now depends also on what the artist wants to paint with. There are different types of paint and they require different types of surfaces.

▲ *Mona Lisa* by Leonardo da Vinci

The three main types of paint are oil, watercolor, and acrylic. Oil paints are stored in tubes and are usually painted onto a surface made of canvas. This is a tough, tightly-woven fabric used for sails and tents as well as for paintings. It is difficult to tear.

Watercolor paints are hard blocks of color that are often stored in a tin. Alternatively, they may be purchased in a tube, squeezed out onto a palette and left to harden. They are usually painted onto paper. To use them the artist adds a little water with a paintbrush to wet the surface of the hard paint. This gives a strong, bright color, when painted onto paper. The more water is added, the thinner the paint will be, so the artist can create a thin, almost transparent "wash."

What kind of paints are sometimes stored in a tin?

ⓐ oil paints   ⓑ watercolor paints

KEY WORDS

- oil
- watercolor
- acrylic
- store
- tough
- tightly-woven
  (*cf.* weave(weave-wove-woven))
- fabric
- sail
- A as well as B
- **tear** (tear-tore-torn)
- block
- tin
- alternatively
- purchase
- squeeze
- **leave** (leave-left-left)
- harden
- thin
- wash

▲ an oil painting on canvas

▲ a watercolor painting on paper

▲ *Jamaica Hut* by William Berryman

This watercolor painting by William Berryman, created in the early 1800s, shows the way in which he first sketched the picture and then began to fill it in with watercolor paints. It was painted in Jamaica and has the simple title, *Jamaica Hut.* But the painting was never finished, so perhaps Berryman might have given it a different title when it was complete. What would you call it if it was your painting?

KEY WORDS

- fill in
- hut
- option
- century

- straight
- thick
- sticky
- nail polish

- remover
- make a mess
  (*cf.* mess / messy)

As well as oil and watercolor paints, there is a third option that the modern artist may choose: acrylic paints. Acrylic paints were invented in the 20th century. They can be used in many different ways, on many different surfaces. Acrylic paints may be mixed with water to make them thinner, like watercolors, or they can be used straight from the tube in their thick, sticky form. Acrylic paints are easy to clean up if they are still wet, because they wash out of clothing or from skin using water. If the paint has dried, it is more difficult, but it can be removed with nail polish remover. Oil paints are much more difficult to remove. So acrylics are good for people who make a mess while they are painting!

Oil paints and acrylics are good for creating a picture with a rough texture. This is done by putting on thick strokes of paint, either with a brush or a flat knife called a palette knife. This can be clearly seen in Vincent van Gogh's oil painting, *The Starry Night*, painted in 1889. The rough texture of the paint makes it look as though the stars are moving and shining.

▲ a self-portrait of Vincent van Gogh

▲ an image of an artist using a palette knife

▲ *The Starry Night* by Vincent van Gogh

Who painted *The Starry Night*?

ⓐ Vincent van Gogh
ⓑ William Berryman

KEY WORDS

- rough
- texture

- put on (put-put-put)
- stroke

- palette knife
- starry

Chapter Two

Comprehension Quiz

A Fill in each blank with the right word below.

blocks	tubes	types	sails

❶ There are three main ________________ of paint.

❷ Oil paints are stored in ________________ .

❸ Canvas is used for ________________ and tents.

❹ A watercolor tin contains ________________ of color.

B Circle the right word for each underlined part.

❶ (Botanical / Abstract) artist Martin J. Allen paints highly detailed paintings of plants.

❷ Artists who paint (still life / abstract) art claim that they get their ideas as they go along.

❸ The artist chooses the (medium / mural) depending on how the finished piece will look, or what message will be given.

❹ Many artists choose to paint on a flat (tube / surface), which can later be hung on a wall for viewing.

 Choose the best answer to each question.

❶ What inspired the "black" paintings of Odilon Redon?

a) his illness

b) his blindness

c) his friendships

d) his dreams and nightmares

❷ Which of these is NOT a type of paint?

a) oil

b) canvas

c) watercolor

d) acrylic

D Mark T for true or F for false.

❶ Acrylic paints were invented in the 19th century.   T   F

❷ Acrylic paints are kept in tubes.   T   F

❸ Acrylic paints can be used on very few surfaces.   T   F

❹ Acrylic paints can be used for creating a picture with a rough texture.   T   F

Painting a Picture

Once the artist has decided what to paint, and which media will be used, it's time to decide *where* to work on the painting. An artist who wishes to paint a landscape may choose to go outside. He or she may sit or stand in front of the view they want to paint. If it is a scene that is unlikely to change over a period of days, and if the weather remains suitable, an artist may complete the whole picture outside.

KEY WORDS

- scene
- be unlikely to + *Verb*
- period
- remain
- suitable

More often, he or she makes
a pencil sketch first, and may
add bits of paint which have
been mixed to the exact shade
required. The artist may take
photographs and add written
notes to the sketch in order
to remember exactly how the
scene looked. Then, the artist
goes back indoors to produce
the actual painting.

Sometimes, an artist works entirely from a photograph. This has
several advantages, such as the fact that the subject will remain
completely the same. If an artist is painting a person or an
animal, it can be easier to copy a photograph. The subject is not
moving, complaining, or changing the way they look from one
day to the next! However, some artists prefer to work from the
original subject — the actual person or animal. They want their
painting to capture the character as well as the way the subject
looks.

KEY WORDS

- more often (than not)
- bits of
- **exact** (*cf.* exactly)
- note
- in order to + *Verb*
- actual
- entirely
- advantage
- complain
- from one day to the next
- prefer
- character

Many artists choose to paint indoors. Some artists use ordinary rooms in their homes. This requires careful thought because not just any room will do.  If an artist is going to paint a large painting, it may be set up on an easel, which takes up a lot of space. There may be a big mess to clean up, and sketches or photographs may be pinned up around the room. The artist needs a place where these things can be left out, rather than having to tidy them away each day.

The room needs plenty of natural light, so large windows are helpful. But light changes throughout the day. A room which receives a lot of warm sunlight in the morning may be darker and dimmer during the afternoon. Changes in light cause changes in the color of the subject and may also cast shadows. For this reason, some artists in the northern hemisphere choose a room that faces north. It receives less sunlight, but the light stays almost the same throughout the day.

KEY WORDS

- **light** (light-lit-lit)
- **throughout**
- **dim** (*cf.* dimly)

- cause
- **cast a shadow** (cast-cast-cast)
- for this reason

- northern
- hemisphere

▲ *The Painter's Studio* by Joos van Craesbeeck

Some artists are lucky enough to have a room that is set aside just for their art, called a studio. They can go into their studio and escape from all the distractions of life to focus on their painting. So what should an artist's studio look like? Leonardo da Vinci said that the studio should be small, to help the artist to concentrate. Not everyone agrees. Pablo Picasso had a huge studio where many of his artworks were kept. He also entertained models and visitors.

Some artists need a big studio because their paintings are big. Jackson Pollock, a U.S. artist who died in 1956, created huge paintings by laying his canvases on the floor and dripping or splashing paint all over them.

▲ Jackson Pollock's studio floor

A studio may not just be for painting. If an artist is going to spend hours working on something, there is often a small kitchen, a sofa or even a bed. Some artists can only work if their studio is tidy. But others are so busy creating that they don't notice the big mess around them.

POP QUIZ

Who created paintings by dripping paint onto canvases on the floor?

ⓐ Pablo Picasso
ⓑ Jackson Pollock

KEY WORDS

- set aside
- studio
- escape
- distraction
- focus on
- concentrate
- entertain
- lay (lay-laid-laid)
- drip
- splash
- notice

▲ a replica of Francis Bacon's studio

Tourists in Dublin, Ireland, can go and visit a replica of the studio belonging to Irish-born painter Francis Bacon, who died in 1992. The floor is covered with tins of paint, photographs, articles cut from newspapers, and all kinds of objects.

Francis Bacon once said that he could not work in places that were too tidy. He found it much easier to paint in a studio that was messy.

Where is the replica of Francis Bacon's studio?
ⓐ Dublin
ⓑ London

KEY WORDS

- replica
- Irish
- article
- be ready to + *Verb*
- professional

- ultramarine
- cobalt blue
- Prussian blue
- pale
- amount

- primary color
- combination
- purple
- aim to + *Verb*
- intense

Prussian	ultramarine	sky	navy
indigo	cobalt	teal	ocean
peacock	azure	cerulean	lapis
spruce	stone	Aegean	berry
denim	admiral	sapphire	Arctic

▲ various shades of blue

Once the artist is ready to begin, he or she must choose which colors to use. Paint colors, whether they are oils, watercolors or acrylics, come in many different shades with interesting names. A professional artist's collection of paints will not simply contain "blue." It might include such exciting names as "ultramarine," "cobalt blue" and "Prussian blue." Of course, an artist may create whatever shades of color he or she wants by mixing paints together. Adding white will make a color paler. Adding tiny amounts of black will make it darker. Mixing the primary colors of red, blue, and yellow together in different combinations will produce shades of purple, orange, and green. Some painters of modern art focus only on one color. They aim to produce a new shade of that color which is particularly beautiful or intense.

The process of painting is different for each artist. Some spend hours getting a very small part of the painting perfect. Others create a general idea of the overall picture and then change parts of it. They add or change colors, and correct mistakes. Some people think that once the painting is done, it cannot be altered, but this is not true. Art historians use the term "pentimento" for paintings which suggest that the artist changed his or her mind about the painting while it was being painted. Sometimes this can be seen by experts, who notice that there are traces of paint which do not seem to match the finished picture. Often, these traces of the original picture are invisible until X-ray or infra-red technology is used to study the painting.

How can we find out "pentimento"?
ⓐ by using paints
ⓑ by using X-ray

KEY WORDS

▪ process	▪ term	▪ match
▪ general	▪ pentimento	▪ invisible (↔ visible)
▪ overall	▪ suggest	▪ infra-red
▪ correct	▪ expert	▪ study
▪ alter	▪ trace	
▪ historian	▪ seem	

▲ *The Syndics of the Amsterdam Drapers* by Rembrandt

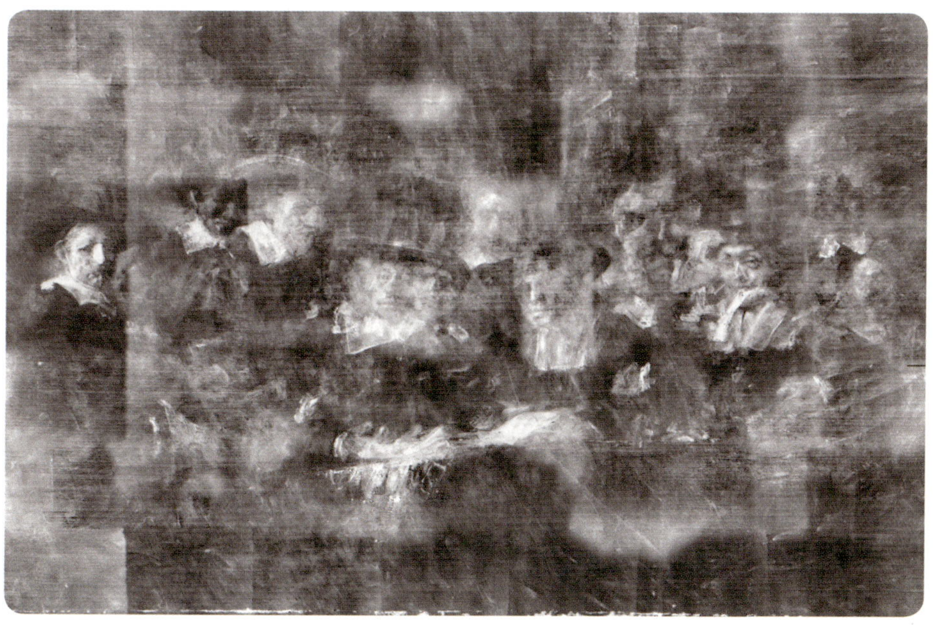

▲ an X-ray image of the painting above shows the painter's early sketches of the composition

▲ *The Arnolfini Portrait* by Jan van Eyck

A good example of this is *The Arnolfini Portrait*. It was painted by Jan van Eyck in 1434. Scientific examination of the portrait has revealed the changes that Jan van Eyck made. The eyes, hands, and feet were originally in different positions. Most of these changes were made when the painting was just an "underdrawing." This means they were made before the paint was added. But some were made during the painting process itself.

KEY WORDS

- underdrawing
- titanium white
- base
- layer
- draw attention to
- linseed oil
- soluble
- lift
- absorbent

Some changes are easier to make than others. When using acrylic paints, an artist can remove as much of the original as possible. Then the area may be painted with titanium white paint. This gives a white base on which to add the new color. With oil

paints, it is not so easy. Adding extra layers of paint may simply draw more attention to a mistake. But oil paint which is not yet dry may be removed using a soft cloth. A little linseed oil may be added to remove the final traces. Watercolor paints are soluble in water, so they can be re-wetted by adding more water. Then, they may be lifted off with an absorbent kitchen paper towel. Once the painting surface is dry again, the artist may continue painting with fresh paint.

How can we change an oil painting?
ⓐ use a soft cloth when it is not yet dry
ⓑ add more water

Comprehension Quiz

A Fill in each blank with the right preposition below.

around	on	in	from

❶ Some artists are so busy creating that they don't notice the mess ______________ them.

❷ The floor is covered with articles cut ______________ newspapers.

❸ Francis Bacon said that he could not work ______________ places that were too tidy.

❹ An artist may spend hours working ______________ something.

B Circle the right word for each underlined part.

❶ Oil paint which is not yet dry may be (painted / completed / removed) using a soft cloth.

❷ Watercolor paints are (soluble / solid / invisible) in water, so they can be re-wetted by adding more water.

❸ Watercolor paints may be lifted off with absorbent kitchen (paper towel / tools / brushes).

❹ Once the painting surface is dry again, the artist may (stop / cease / continue) painting with fresh paint.

C Choose the best answer to each question.

❶ Why is it an advantage to paint from a photograph instead of a real, living subject?

a) The artist can see more detail.

b) The painting is more realistic.

c) The subject is not moving.

d) The colors can be matched more accurately.

❷ As well as painting, what did Pablo Picasso do in his studio?

a) He framed pictures for other people.

b) He laid out all his canvases on the floor.

c) He entertained models and visitors.

d) He sold tickets for the public to come and view it.

D Complete each sentence by connecting the first part to its related second part.

❶ An artist may create •   • a) focus only on one color.

❷ Some painters of •   • b) whatever shades of color
modern art   he or she wants.

❸ Some artists spend •   • c) a very small part of the
hours getting   painting perfect.

The Finished Painting

At last, the painting is complete! Now, many more people with different jobs are needed to take the painting further on its journey.

The next stage is usually framing. This may be done by the artist if she or he knows how, but is often done by a picture framer. There are two main reasons for framing a finished painting. The first is to make it look attractive. The second is to protect it from damage.

Most paintings are displayed within a frame, but some modern canvases are displayed without a frame. This means that the sides of the painting are visible.

Paintings done on paper or board are framed for support. Many paintings on canvas are framed, too. A canvas must first be stretched over wooden bars called stretcher bars, and

▲ a canvas fastened to the sides of the stretcher bars

the painting is fastened to the sides of the bars. Paper is much more fragile than canvas. It is usually mounted on some kind of board before framing, to prevent tearing or other damage.

POP QUIZ

Name the bars used in preparing a canvas for framing.

ⓐ gallery bars
ⓑ stretcher bars

KEY WORDS

- **further**
- **stage**
- **frame** (*cf.* framer)
- **attractive**
- **damage**

- **board** (= cardboard)
- **support**
- **stretch**
- **stretcher**
- **fasten**

- **fragile**
- **mount** (= attach)
- **prevent**

Often, a painting is framed behind glass, especially if it is painted on paper. Glass keeps the painting in good condition by protecting it from dust or chemicals in the air. It prevents people from touching the painting. It also reduces the amount of light — especially ultraviolet light — that reaches the painting. Although light is needed to view the painting and to appreciate its colors, too much light can damage the painting. This is why many art galleries are dimly lit.

POP QUIZ

What kind of light damages paintings most?

ⓐ ultraviolet light
ⓑ blue light

KEY WORDS

- dust
- chemical
- reduce
- ultraviolet light
- reach
- appreciate

Oil paintings do not need glass to protect them. Instead, a layer of transparent varnish is added on top of the painting. This is where an artist needs to be very patient. An oil painting must only be varnished six months after it has been completed! This is to make sure that the paint is completely dry. If the paint is very thick, the artist must wait even longer. If the varnish is added too soon, the varnish will dry before the paint does. After a while, cracks will appear on the surface. The painting will be worthless and the artist will find it difficult to make any money from it. Occasionally, oil paintings are framed under glass, particularly in museums and art galleries. This is usually to give protection to very valuable paintings that may be damaged by members of the public.

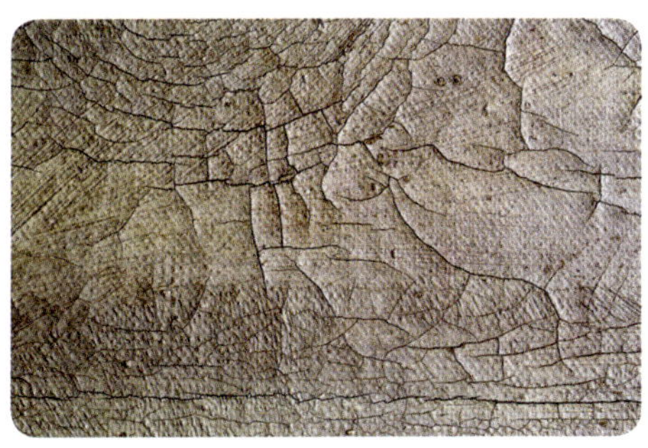

▲ cracks on the surface of an oil painting

The next decision is what kind of frame to use. Some frames
are very thin and plain. Others are extremely elaborate, and are
carved or molded into fancy shapes. Frames are traditionally
made of wood, but in modern times they may also be made of
metal or certain plastics. Some frames are "gilded." This means
that they are made to look as though they are made of gold.
This can be done by painting them with gold paint or by adding
gold leaf. Gold leaf is an extremely thin layer of real gold, added
little by little with a fine brush.

▲ gold leaf used for the frames

▲ an image of gilding a frame

- plain
- extremely
- elaborate
- carve (into)
- mold
- fancy
- traditionally
- metal
- certain
- gild
- gold leaf
- fine

When the framing is complete,
the painting is ready to be
displayed and put up for sale.
At this point, the artist may
need the help of several people.
They can help to sell his or
her paintings and to reach the

widest audience. Of course, artists can sell their own work. But
it takes a lot of time and effort that could be used for painting
more pictures. For this reason, many artists choose to use the
services of an agent.

An art agent is someone who works on behalf of artists to get
their work displayed in the right places and sold to the right
people. The agent is usually someone who has many years of
experience in the art world. The agent has a lot of connections
with buyers, galleries and auction houses (which we will talk
about in the next chapter).

POP QUIZ

What is correct about an art agent?

ⓐ An art agent sells his or her own paintings.
ⓑ An art agent has many years of experience in the art world.

KEY WORDS

- put up for sale
- audience
- agent
- on behalf of
- connection
- auction house

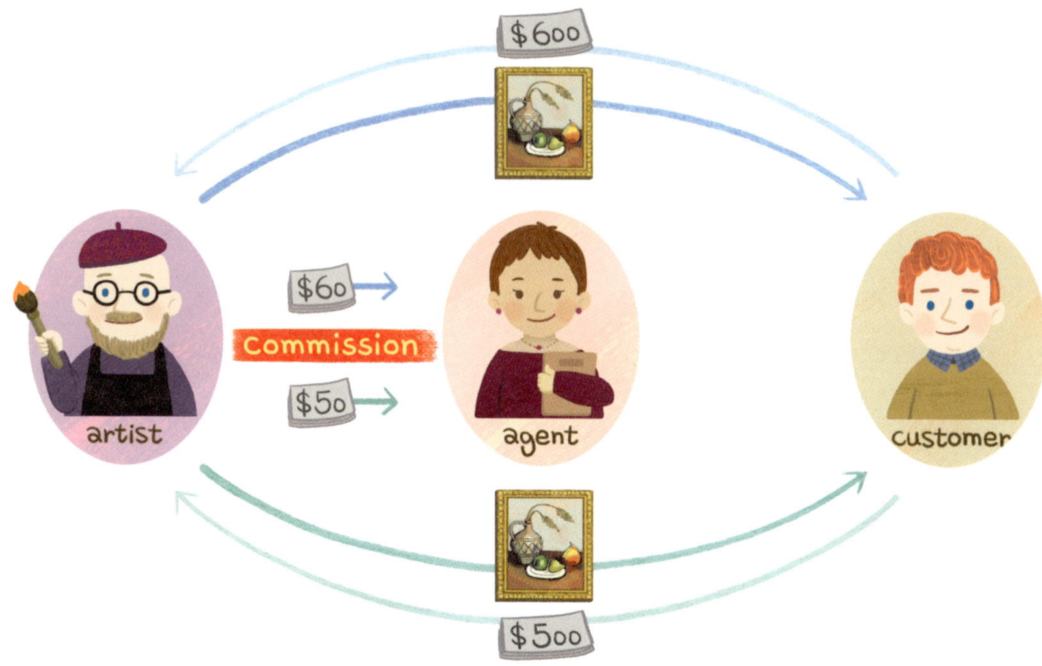

The agent makes his or her money by taking a percentage
of the money that the artist earns. This is called working for
"commission." It means that the more money the artist makes,
the more money the agent makes! Some agents, instead of
working on behalf of the artist, work on behalf of a gallery. They
look around for suitable artworks to display and sell. They may
contact artists to ask if they have any work currently ready
to display. Many agents who work this way are experts in a
particular style of art. They often travel all over the world to find
new and exciting artists.

Artists who are already quite well-known and successful may use the services of an art manager. Many musicians such as pop stars use managers to arrange everything in their careers. The art manager does a similar thing for the artist. The manager takes care of all the artist's business. Money management, marketing, and publicity events are some of the things a manager may take care of.

Of course, an artist who is just beginning a career in painting may not have an agent, and certainly will not have a manager. The artist needs to get his or her paintings in front of people who may enjoy looking at them and may even want to buy them. The best way to do this is to hold an exhibition in an art gallery.

KEY WORDS

- earn
- commission
- contact
- currently

- career
- similar
- management
- marketing

- publicity
- event
- hold an exhibition

Comprehension Quiz

A Match the two sides to correctly complete each sentence.

❶ An artist   •   • a) displays the picture to the public.

❷ An agent   •   • b) manages the artist's business.

❸ An art manager •   • c) paints the picture.

❹ A gallery   •   • d) tries to sell work for a commission.

B Fill in each blank with the right word below.

worthless	suitable	visible	transparent

❶ When canvases are displayed without a frame, the sides are ______________.

❷ A layer of ______________ varnish is added on top of oil paintings.

❸ A painting with cracks on the surface will be ______________.

❹ Art agents look around for ______________ artworks to display and sell.

C Choose the best answer to each question.

❶ What is a "gilded" frame?

a) a frame that is thin and plain

b) a frame that is carved from one piece of wood

c) a frame that is made of pure gold

d) a frame that is made to look as though it is made of gold

❷ Why do many artists choose NOT to sell their own work by themselves?

a) They would rather spend their time painting.

b) They do not think it is good enough to sell.

c) They are not interested in making money.

d) They do not know anyone to sell it to.

D Mark T for true or F for false.

❶ All agents work on behalf of an artist.   T   F

❷ An agent usually has a lot of experience in the art world.   T   F

❸ Many agents travel all over the world.   T   F

❹ The less money an artist makes, the more money an agent makes.   T   F

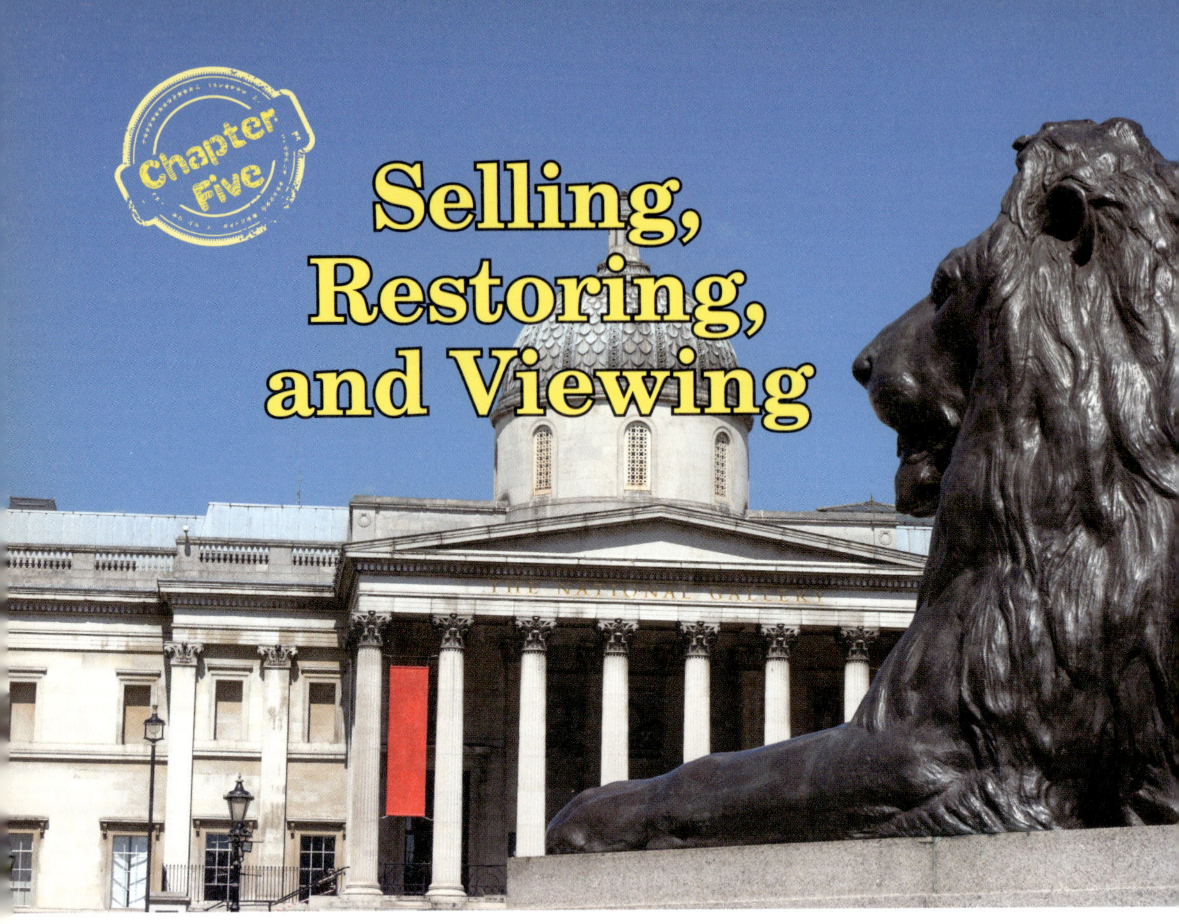

Selling, Restoring, and Viewing

Galleries are rooms or buildings with plenty of space for displaying artworks such as paintings. They are open to allow viewers to come and look at the paintings. Even the fictional spy James Bond visits art galleries! In the 2012 movie, *Skyfall*, James Bond meets his boss, Q, in the National Gallery, London.

KEY WORDS

▪ fictional   ▪ boss   ▪ national

The same gallery features in the 2007 movie, *St. Trinian's*, about a group of very naughty schoolgirls who steal a famous painting called *Girl with a Pearl Earring*. This is a public gallery, where the work is not for sale. Smaller galleries hold special events or exhibitions, where the work of a particular artist may be displayed and offered for sale.

▲ *Girl with a Pearl Earring* by Johannes Vermeer

Usually, there is a special event on the first night of the exhibition. The artist attends, along with invited guests who may buy the paintings. Food and drink are usually served, and it is an exciting social occasion.

If an artist exhibits his or her work in a gallery, hopefully people will come and buy the work. Sometimes, they do not buy the work immediately, especially if the price is high. The artist needs a catalog. This is a glossy magazine-style book with images of the paintings in it, and details of prices. Customers may take these catalogs away and take time to make their decision.

Some customers may want to buy a painting simply because they like looking at it, and would love to see it hanging in their home. Other customers buy a painting because they collect art and they see it as an investment. This means that they will only buy a painting that they think will be worth even more money in the future. Such customers will be especially interested in finding out more about the artist. They have to decide whether to invest in both the artist and the work. For this reason, artists who are serious about making a living from their painting need to have a website. Here, they can give information about themselves and their work.

There is another important job in the art world, which helps customers to decide whether to buy a painting or not. This is the job of the art critic. 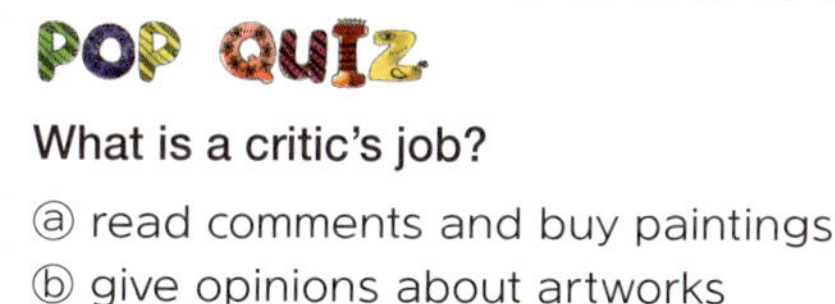 An art critic is someone who looks at art and thinks about how well it has been painted. Critics give their opinions about all kinds of artworks. They write about art in magazines, newspapers, exhibition catalogs, and websites. Customers read the comments written by critics. They use the comments to help with the decision about what to buy.

POP QUIZ

What is a critic's job?

ⓐ read comments and buy paintings
ⓑ give opinions about artworks

KEY WORDS

- immediately
- glossy
- make one's decision
- investment

- worth
- find out
- invest in
- serious

- make a living
- critic
- opinion
- comment

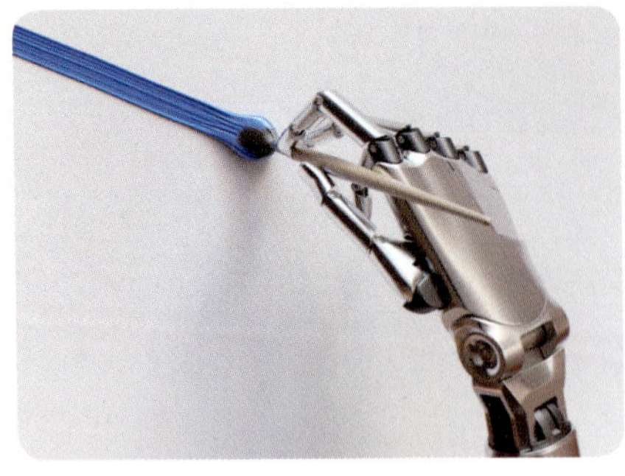

An unusual task for art critics took place in 2016 for the first time, when some critics judged the entries in the first annual robotic art competition. Open to teams from all over the world, this competition offers prizes worth $100,000 for artworks produced by robots! Robots can paint in two ways. Humans may operate a robotic arm using a remote control, or the robot may be controlled using computer software. One of the simplest techniques is for the robot to copy a photograph or painting. It paints one color at a time, so, for example, all the red parts of the picture may be painted first. Then, all the blue parts, the yellow parts, and so on. In this way, the picture is slowly built up.

KEY WORDS

- take place
- judge
- entry
- annual
- competition
- offer
- operate
- remote control
- and so on (= and so forth)
- build up

Another way of selling paintings is through art "auction houses."
Auction houses sell all kinds of items. In galleries, the price of
a painting is fixed. An auction is different. It is a special type
of sale where people decide what they would like to pay. An
expert seller called an "auctioneer" displays the painting to a

gathered crowd. The auctioneer
asks what people would like to
offer, or "bid." People who are
interested in buying the painting
raise their hand or nod their
head. This tells the auctioneer
that they want to compete with
the other buyers.

Who sells the paintings at an auction house?

ⓐ a bidder

ⓑ an auctioneer

KEY WORDS

- fixed
- auctioneer
- gather

- crowd
- **bid** (bid-bid-bid)
- raise one's hand

- nod one's head
- compete with

Each time, the bid increases and the price of the painting goes up. As the price gets higher, some bidders drop out of the competition. The auctioneer continues to ask for bids until only two or three bidders are left. Eventually, the painting is sold to the person who bids the highest price.

Two of the most famous art auction houses in the world are Christie's and Sotheby's.  They sell all kinds of art that you can imagine. Both of these auction houses operate all over the world, with famous salesrooms in London and New York.

In 2010, a painting by Pablo Picasso called *Nude, Green Leaves and Bust* was offered for sale by Christie's. It was sold in 8 minutes for the incredible sum of $106.5 million. Picasso painted this picture in a single day. That's a good rate of pay for one day's work! Picasso was wealthy when he died. But he'd still be amazed at that rate of pay.

POP QUIZ

Where was *Nude, Green Leaves and Bust* sold?
ⓐ Christie's
ⓑ Sotheby's

KEY WORDS

- bidder
- drop out of
- eventually
- salesroom
- bust
- sum
- in a single day
- rate of pay
- be amazed at

◀ Sotheby's in London

▼ an image of a Sotheby's art auction

An auction house, however, is not a place where new artists generally sell their paintings. Many of the paintings sold at auction houses are by well-known artists. Sometimes, customers may build up a collection of paintings over many years as an investment. Then, they may sell some or all of their paintings at auction houses to make money. Two men called

▲ a still life painting by Juan Gris

Ezra and David Nahmad own the most valuable art collection in the world. It is valued at around $3 billion! Their collection is stored in a warehouse near Geneva airport, in Switzerland. This suggests that they do not buy the art because they love to look at it. However, they make a lot of money from it and are the most frequent sellers of art at Christie's in New York.

KEY WORDS

- generally
- be valued at
- billion

- warehouse
- frequent
- billionaire

- lend out (lend-lent-lent)
- hide away
- bring out

▲ Eli and Edythe Broad Art Museum

Another great art collector is an American billionaire called Eli Broad, who owns 8,000 artworks. 🌐 He wants these to be enjoyed by as many people as possible, so he lends out his paintings to galleries, museums, and universities.

So, in the same way that art is created for many different reasons, it is also bought for different reasons. How do artists feel when the painting that they have worked so hard on is hidden away and only brought out to make money? It is difficult to know, since many of the paintings which sell for the highest amounts are by artists who died many years ago. Fortunately, many of them are displayed for anyone to see in public art galleries.

Some of the paintings displayed in public galleries are centuries old. They need the attention of some more important people in the art world. These people are curators and conservators. The art curator's job is to create and care for a collection of art for public display. The curator of a major public gallery decides which paintings to buy. He or she also decides which ones to hang on the walls, which to store carefully for a while, and which to lend to other galleries. The curator's job includes keeping careful records about the paintings. It also includes producing labels, written information, and catalog entries.

- curator
- conservator
- care for
- major
- label
- catalog entry
- security guard
- get rid of
- accidentally
- ruin
- horrified
- lose (lose-lost-lost)
- be responsible for

The 1997 comedy movie, *Bean*, features the curator of an art gallery in Los Angeles, whose name is David Langley. David believes Mr. Bean is a famous art critic sent by the National Gallery in London. So he invites him to stay at his house. But the National Gallery only sent Mr. Bean, a security guard, to get rid of him. When Mr. Bean accidentally ruins a famous and valuable painting called *Whistler's Mother,* David is horrified. He knows that he may lose his job, since he is responsible for taking care of the paintings. Being a curator is a very responsible job!

▲ *Whistler's Mother* by James Whistler

The work of art conservators is more technical. Firstly, they conserve art. This means that they protect it against harm or damage. They try to keep it as close to its original condition as possible. They also repair artworks which have been damaged.

They are restored — brought back — to their original condition. The damage may have been done by age or by environmental issues such as water or light. Sometimes the restoration of a painting might actually cause more damage. Even if the restoration is carefully carried out, people might not like the result. Aha!

KEY WORDS

- technical
- conserve
- harm
- close

- repair
- **restore** (*cf.* restoration)
- bring back
- environmental

- issue
- carry out

Art restoration should only be done by experts. In a small town in Spain called Zaragoza, there is a church with a fresco, which is a wall painting. The fresco is a painting of Jesus, and it is hundreds of years old. An eighty-year-old woman in the town noticed that white patches had developed on the face of Jesus, so she decided to fix it herself. She painted a new face of Jesus over the old one. Unfortunately, the new face looked completely different! But it is now a popular tourist attraction.

KEY WORDS

▪ fresco   ▪ patch   ▪ tourist attraction

When a painting is correctly restored, there is often a lot of
science involved. Lasers can be used to remove dirt. They heat
and expand the surface layer. This creates a wave of pressure
which lifts dirt off the surface. The laser beam is only used for
short amounts of time — often less than one second — but
it is very powerful. Some art restorers use bacteria to clean

paintings. Certain bacteria
produce chemicals called
enzymes. The enzymes
break down dirt and lift it off
the surface of the painting
without causing any damage.

Now the journey of the painting is at an end. It has been painted, framed, sold, and displayed so that many people may enjoy looking at it. Why not take a trip to an art gallery to view some paintings? Or why not try painting a picture yourself and having it framed? Next time you look at a painting, think about all the people that have been involved in creating it. But most of all, look at it with enjoyment. See if you can guess the message that the artist wanted to give. That message has traveled a long way to reach you!

Comprehension Quiz

A Which place does the following sentence explain? Choose and circle.

❶ The price of a painting is fixed.

GALLERY / AUCTION HOUSE

❷ People who want to buy a painting make a bid.

GALLERY / AUCTION HOUSE

❸ Customers must decide at once whether to buy a painting.

GALLERY / AUCTION HOUSE

❹ Customers may decide to buy a painting at a later date.

GALLERY / AUCTION HOUSE

B Which job does the following sentence explain? Choose and circle.

❶ Produces labels and written information about paintings.

CURATOR / CONSERVATOR

❷ Repairs artworks that have been damaged.

CURATOR / CONSERVATOR

❸ Uses science to restore paintings to their original condition.

CURATOR / CONSERVATOR

❹ Decides which painting to hang on the walls.

CURATOR / CONSERVATOR

C Choose the best answer to each question.

❶ How do customers at an auction show that they want to make a bid?

a) They press buttons on a computer.

b) They raise their hands or nod their heads.

c) They call out the price they want to pay.

d) They stand up.

❷ Where do Ezra and David Nahmad store their art collection?

a) in a bank

b) in a warehouse

c) in a gallery

d) in a basement

D Fill in each blank with the right word below.

invited	social	first	smaller

❶ ______________ galleries hold special events and exhibitions.

❷ Usually, there is a special event on the ____________ night of an exhibition.

❸ The artist attends, along with ____________ guests.

❹ This is an exciting ____________ occasion.

Let's Review the Story

Fill in the blanks to review the story.

Title:

Chapter 1

People create art for different reasons, e.g:

- to show which t__________ they belong to
- to make m__________
- to pass on a m__________

Chapter 2

Artists may use three different types of paint, which are:

- o__________
- w__________
- a__________

Chapter 3

Many artists work on their paintings in a s__________. This needs plenty of n__________ l__________. There may be a kitchen and a sofa or even a bed.

Chapter 4

Artists needs the help of other people:

- F__________ frame paintings to p__________ them and to make them look a__________.
- A__________ help artists to s__________ their artworks, and receive c__________ as payment.

Chapter 5

When paintings are sold, more people get involved:

- C__________ write about their o__________ of artworks.
- C__________ take care of art collections in public g__________.
- C__________ protect and r__________ paintings to their original condition.

Let's Think & Talk

Think about the following questions and answer them freely.

❶ Do you like to appreciate works of art or create them for yourself? Why or why not?

❷ In the book, various people related to works of art are introduced. Tell us how a painter, an art agent, a manager, an art critic, an auctioneer, a collector, a curator and an art restorer are different.

❸ Besides the painter, which job is the most important in order to create a masterpiece? Why?

❹ Among the works of art by many painters introduced in the book, which one impresses you the most? Tell us why you think so.

Let's Review the Story

Title: Things to Know about Paintings

Chapter 1

People create art for different reasons, e.g:
- to show which **tribe** they belong to
- to make **money**
- to pass on a **message**

Chapter 2

Artists may use three different types of paint, which are:
- **oil**
- **watercolor**
- **acrylic**

Chapter 3

Many artists work on their paintings in a **studio**. This needs plenty of **natural** **light**. There may be a kitchen and a sofa or even a bed.

Chapter 4

Artists needs the help of other people:
- **Framers** frame paintings to **protect** them and to make them look **attractive**.
- **Agents** help artists to **sell** their artworks, and receive **commissions** as payment.

Chapter 5

When paintings are sold, more people get involved:
- **Critics** write about their **opinions** of artworks.
- **Curators** take care of art collections in public **galleries**.
- **Conservators** protect and **restore** paintings to their original condition.

After-reading Test

- **Things to Know about Paintings**
- **Level 6**
- **25 Questions**

  (Vocabulary 6 / Reading Comprehension 16 /

  Sentence Structure & Grammar 3)

1. What is an art "installation"?
   ① art that hangs on a wall
   ② art that is a performance
   ③ art that is made for people to wear
   ④ art that has no title

2. What does "hovering" mean in the following sentence?

   Guardian Spirit of the Waters shows a face <u>hovering</u> over the sea.

   ① looking   ② floating
   ③ threatening   ④ guarding

3. What does "fragile" mean?
   ① white   ② useful
   ③ delicate   ④ cheap

4. What is the right word for the blank?

   Sometimes, customers may build up a collection of paintings over many years as a(n) ____________.

   ① communication
   ② commission
   ③ responsibility
   ④ investment

5. What is the common word for the two blanks?

> If an artist is going to paint a large painting, it may be set ____________ on an easel, which takes ____________ a lot of space.

① on

② up

③ out

④ with

6. What are the proper words for the blanks?

> - When the framing is complete, the painting is ready to be displayed and put ____________ for sale.
> - The art curator's job is to create and care ____________ a collection of art for public display.

① to – of

② up – for

③ to – of

④ up – in

7. Why are most cave paintings painted using red, black, brown, or yellowish colors?

① People did not like other colors in those days.

② The colors were made using earth and rocks.

③ A wide range of colors were used, but time has changed them all to dull colors.

④ Green and blue colors were spoiled because people painted with dirty fingers.

8. What is recorded in the painting *Guernica*?

① the beauty of Spanish scenery

② the shape of Spanish buildings

③ the suffering of Spanish people

④ the variety of Spanish animals

9. What message did Picasso want to give people in his painting, *Guernica*?
① War is exciting.
② War is a bad thing.
③ War doesn't happen anymore.
④ War helps people to be brave.

10. What does a botanical artist paint?
① animals   ② plants
③ insects   ④ people

11. What type of art consists of patterns, shapes, and lines without an obvious picture?
① abstract art   ② acrylic art
③ street art   ④ cave art

12. What is a "mural"?
① a painting on canvas
② a painting on paper
③ a painting on wood
④ a painting on a building

13. What does "trompe l'oeil" mean?
① mistake of the eye
② picture on the ground
③ painting done with oils
④ moving picture

14. Why might a landscape artist write on his or her sketch?

   ① to instruct people how to draw it

   ② to make notes about how the scene looked

   ③ to prove the identity of the artist

   ④ to send it as a gift

15. Why do some artists choose to paint the original subject instead of using a photograph of the subject?

   ① They prefer to paint quickly.

   ② They prefer to capture the character of the subject.

   ③ They prefer to paint outdoors.

   ④ They prefer to move around while they paint.

16. What are the "primary colors"?

   ① black and white

   ② orange, green, and purple

   ③ red, blue, and yellow

   ④ brown and gray

17. What kind of paintings does the word "pentimento" describe?

   ① paintings which have been painted over a hundred years ago

   ② paintings which use rough strokes of a brush or palette knife

   ③ paintings which show that the artist has changed his or her mind during the process

   ④ paintings which are completely perfect in every way

18. Which of these does NOT damage paintings?

   ① darkness   ② dust

   ③ chemicals   ④ light

19. How does an art agent get paid?
   ① The artist pays the agent a fee each month.
   ② The gallery pays the agent for permission to hold an exhibition.
   ③ The agent receives a percentage of the money that the artist earns.
   ④ The buyers pay the agent a fixed amount for each painting they buy.

20. Which of these is NOT the job of an art critic?
   ① An art critic looks at art and thinks about how well it has been painted.
   ② An art critic gives his or her opinion about all kinds of artworks.
   ③ An art critic writes about art in magazines and newspapers.
   ④ An art critic paints pictures and displays them in galleries.

21. Why does Eli Broad lend his art collection to public galleries, museums, and universities?
   ① He wants lots of people to enjoy looking at the art.
   ② He wants everyone to know what a generous person he is.
   ③ He wants to make money from people paying to display his art.
   ④ He wants to avoid the cost of storing his huge collection.

22. Why did the old woman in Zaragoza decide to paint over the original fresco?
   ① She saw that the original painting was damaged.
   ② She didn't like the way Jesus' face had been painted.
   ③ She wanted to create a new tourist attraction.
   ④ She thought that she could do a better job than the original artist.

※ Choose the wrong part of each sentence. (23~24)

23. This <u>requires</u> careful thought <u>because</u> not just <u>any</u> room will <u>done</u>.
       ①   ②   ③   ④

24. This is <u>to</u> <u>making</u> sure <u>that</u> the paint is <u>completely</u> dry.
      ① ②   ③   ④

25. What is the correct word for the blank?

Sadly, many artists do not become famous ___________ after they are dead.

① so   ② as
③ until   ④ rather

[Image Credit]

p.6   Bisonte Magdaleniense negro

By Museo de Altamira y D. Rodriguez [CC BY–SA 3.0 (http://creativecommons.org/licenses/by-sa/3.0)], via Wikimedia Commons

p.11   A gallery in Tate Modern

By Arpingstone [Public domain], via Wikimedia Commons

p.17   Portrait of Henry VIII of England

By Hans Holbein the Younger (1497/1498 – 1543) [Public domain], via Wikimedia Commons

p.25   A still life painting

By Jan Brueghel the Elder [Public domain], via Wikimedia Commons

p.26   *Mound of Butter*

By Antoine Vallon Antoine Vollon [Public domain], via Wikimedia Commons

L'Illustration horticole

By Lemaire, Charles Antoine (http://www.biodiversitylibrary.org/pageimage/92317) [Public domain], via Wikimedia Commons

p.27   *Guardian Spirit of the Waters*, 1878

By Odilon Redon [Public domain], via Wikimedia Commons

Mon portrait, 1867

By Odilon Redon [Public domain], via Wikimedia Commons

p.28   *Composition No 4*, 1911

By Wm M. Martin vasily kandinsky (http://masterpieceart.net/vasily–kandinsky/) [Public domain], via Wikimedia Commons

p.32   *Rat Photographer*

By Szater (Own work) [Public domain], via Wikimedia Commons

p.33   *Mona Lisa*

By Leonardo da Vinci [Public domain or Public domain], via Wikimedia Commons

p.36   *Jamaica Hut*

By William Berryman (Library of Congress[1]) [Public domain], via Wikimedia Commons

p.38   *Self–portrait*

By Vincent van Gogh [Public domain], via Wikimedia Commons

p.39   *The Starry Night*

By Vincent van Gogh [Public domain], via Wikimedia Commons

p.46   *The Painter's Studio*

By Joos van Craesbeeck [Public domain or Public domain], via Wikimedia Commons

p.47   Studio floor used by Jackson Pollock at Pollock–Krasner House and Study Center in Springs, New York

By Rhododendrites (Own work) [CC BY–SA 4.0 (http://creativecommons.org/licenses/by-sa/4.0)], via Wikimedia Commons

p.48   Francis Bacon's studio at the City Gallery *The Hugh Lane*, Dublin, Ireland

By antomoro (Own work) [FAL or FAL], via Wikimedia Commons

p.51   *The Syndics of the Amsterdam Drapers' Guild*
By Rembrandt [Public domain], via Wikimedia Commons
Rembrandt painting X-Rayed
By Rembrandt [Public domain or Public domain], via Wikimedia Commons

p.52   *The Arnolfini Portrait*
By Jan van Eyck [Public domain], via Wikimedia Commons

p.67   *Girl with a Pearl Earring*
By Johannes Vermeer [Public domain], via Wikimedia Commons

p.73   **Sotheby's in London**
By Dirk Ingo Franke (Own work) [CC BY-SA 3.0 (http://creativecommons.org/licenses/by-sa/3.0)], via Wikimedia Commons
Sotheby's Auction 2016
By Artero113 (Own work) [CC BY-SA 4.0 (http://creativecommons.org/licenses/by-sa/4.0)], via Wikimedia Commons

p.74   *Still Life with Checked Tablecloth*
By Juan Gris [CC0], via Wikimedia Commons

p.75   **MSU Eli and Edythe Broad Art Museum**
By Dj1997 (Own work) [CC BY-SA 3.0 (http://creativecommons.org/licenses/by-sa/3.0)], via Wikimedia Commons

p.77   *Whistler's Mother*
By James Abbott McNeill Whistler [Public domain], via Wikimedia Commons

p.81   **View of the second floor galleries at the Smithsonian American Art Museum**
By Amy Vaughters, Smithsonian American Art Museum (Smithsonian American Art Museum) [CC BY-SA 3.0 (http://creativecommons.org/licenses/by-sa/3.0)], via Wikimedia Commons

* Others are from shutterstock.com.

Sarah J. Dodd
Sarah J. Dodd is an experienced primary school teacher who resides in the UK, but has also lived and taught in Australia. She has a PhD in Science and a certificate in Creative Writing. She has published several books for children: "An Angel Anyway" (Anyway Press, 2008), the "Little Angels" series (Lion Children's Books, 2009/10), "The Lion Picture Bible" (Lion Children's Books, 2015) and "Legs: the tale of a meerkat lost and found" (Lion Children's Books, 2015). Her poetry for children has also been highly commended and published in the anthology "Let in the Stars" (Manchester Metropolitan University, 2014).
She is currently working on further picture books for the very young, and a novel for older children.

Things to Know about Paintings

Written by Sarah J. Dodd
Illustrated by Sunghee Lee

First Published in August 2017

Editorial Manager: Juyon Choi
Editors: Juyon Choi, Kyunghee Jang, Jiyeong Park
Designer: Eunhee Lee
Cover Designer: Eunhee Lee

Published and distributed by

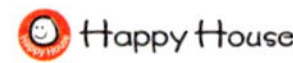

Darakwon Bldg., 64-1 Jandari-ro, Mapo-gu, Seoul, Korea 04031
Tel: 82-2-736-2031(ext. 250)   Fax: 82-2-732-2037
Homepage: www.ihappyhouse.co.kr
Publisher: Kyudo Chung

ISBN: 978-89-6653-548-4 18740 / 978-89-6653-156-1 18740(set)

[Components]
• 1 Audio CD (Recording Studio: Aram)
• Answer Keys & Korean Translation: Free download at www.ihappyhouse.co.kr